2004

ISBN 0-634-08611-1

HAL•LEONARD® CORPORATION

7777 W. BLUEMOUND RD. P.O. BOX 13819 MILWAUKEE, WI 53213

Visit Hal Leonard Online at
www.halleonard.com

ACCIDENTALLY IN LOVE

from the Motion Picture SHREK 2

Words and Music by ADAM DURITZ,
DAN VICKREY, DAVID IMMERGLUCK,
MATTHEW MALLEY and DAVID BRYSON

DON'T TELL ME

Words and Music by AVRIL LAVIGNE
and EVAN TAUBENFELD

BREATHE

Words and Music by RYAN JORDAN,
MARC WANNINGER, ANDREW DWIGGINS,
DOUGLAS RANDALL and BRANDON ARMSTRONG

I played the fool to-day ___ and

I just dream of van-ish-ing in-to ___ the

crowd. Long-ing for ___ home a-gain, ___ but home is a

BURN

Words and Music by USHER RAYMOND,
JERMAINE DUPRI and BRYAN MICHAEL COX

Moderately, with a groove

* Recorded a half step lower

** Vocal written at pitch.

way I feel. __ I knew I made a mis - take. Now it's too late. __ I know she ain't com - in' back. __

__ What I got - ta do now to get my short - y back? __ Ooh, ooh ooh,

ooh, man I don't know what I'm gon - na do with - out my

boo. __ You been gone for too long. __ It's been

EVERYTHING

Words and Music by
ALANIS MORISSETTE

THE FIRST CUT IS THE DEEPEST

Words and Music by
CAT STEVENS

HERE WITHOUT YOU

Words and Music by BRAD ARNOLD,
MATTHEW DARRICK ROBERTS, CHRISTOPHER LEE HENDERSON
and ROBERT TODD HARRELL

*Recorded a half step lower.

HEY YA!

Words and Music by
ANDRE BENJAMIN

One, two, three, uhh. My ba-by don't mess a-round_ be-cause she

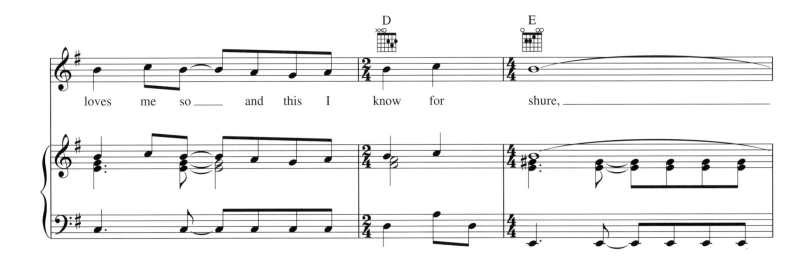

loves me so ___ and this I know for shure, _____

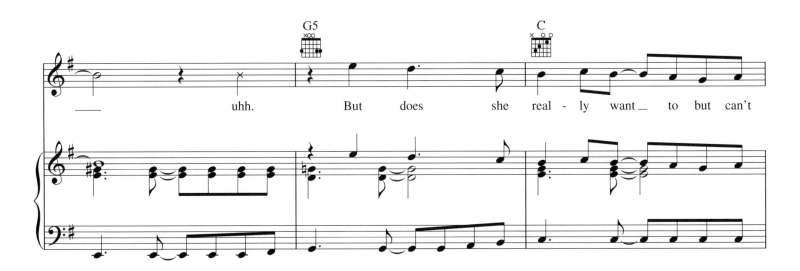

___ uhh. But does she real-ly want_ to but can't

Rap 1: *(See rap lyrics)*

Rap Lyrics

Rap 1: (3000): Hey, alright now. Alright now fellas!
(Fellas): Yeah!
(3000): Now, what's cooler than being cool?
(Fellas): Ice Cold!!!!
(3000): I can't hear ya. I say what's, what's cooler than being cool?
(Fellas): Ice Cold!!!!
(3000): Alright, alright, alright, alright, alright, alright, alright, alright.
Ok, now ladies.
(Ladies): Yeah!!!!
(3000): Now, we gon' break this thing down in just a few seconds.
Now, don't have me break this thing down for nothin'.
Now, I wanna see y'all on y'all baddest behavior.
Lend me some sugar, I am your neighbor, ahh. Here we go, uhh.

Rap 2: Now, all Beyonces and Lucy Lius and Baby Dolls get on the floor.
You know what to do. You know what to do. You know what to do.

I DON'T WANNA KNOW

Words and Music by EITHNE NI BHRAONAIN, NICKY RYAN,
ROMA RYAN, MARIO WINANS, MICHAEL JONES,
CHAUNCEY HAWKINS, ERICK SERMON and PARRISH SMITH

Moderately, with a groove

(Spoken:) I just can't believe this mess.

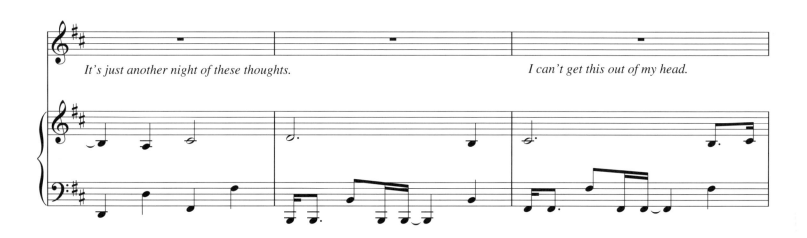

It's just another night of these thoughts.   *I can't get this out of my head.*

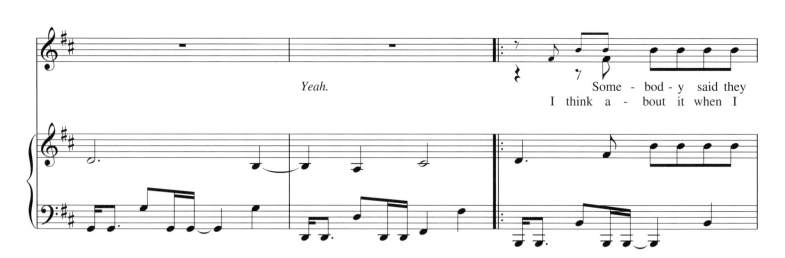

Yeah.

Some - bod - y said they
I think a - bout it when I

creep - in', please don't let it show. Oh, ____

ba - by, I don't wan - na know.

Rap Lyrics

I don't wanna know where your whereabouts or how you movin'.
I know when you in the house or when you cruisin'.
It's been proven, my love you abusin'.
I can't understand how a man got you choosin'.
Undecided, I came and provided my undivided. You came and denied it.
Don't even try it, I know when you lyin'.
Don't even do that, I know why you cryin'.
I'm not applyin' no pressure, just wanna let you know that I don't wanna let you go.
And I don't wanna let you leave.
Can't say I didn't let you breathe, gave you extra cheese. Put you in the SUV.
You wanted ice so I made you freeze.
Made you hot like the West Indies.
Now it's time you invest in me 'cause if not then it's best you leave.
Holla, Yeah.

I WANT YOU

Words and Music by HAROLD LILLY, JR., KANYE WEST,
BURT BACHARACH and HAL DAVID

IF I AIN'T GOT YOU

Words and Music by
ALICIA KEYS

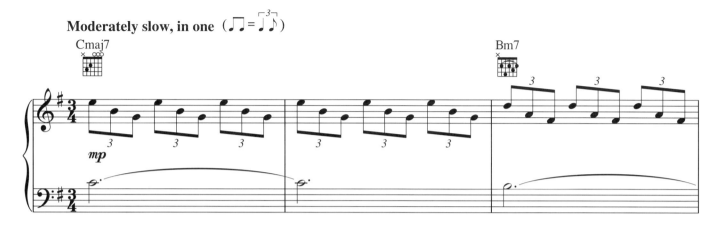

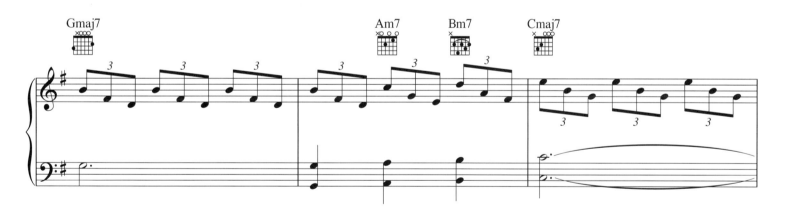

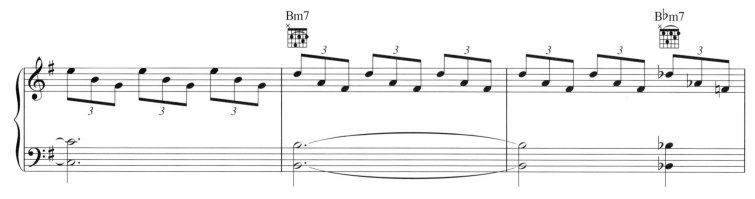

IT'S MY LIFE

Words and Music by MARK DAVID HOLLIS
and TIM FRIESE-GREENE

Recorded a half step lower.

I've asked __ my - self, __ how __ much do __ you _____

MEANT TO LIVE

Words and Music by JONATHAN FOREMAN
and TIM FOREMAN

STACY'S MOM

Words and Music by CHRIS COLLINGWOOD
and ADAM SCHLESINGER

100 YEARS

Words and Music by
JOHN ONDRASIK

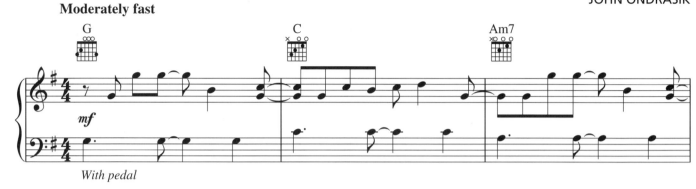

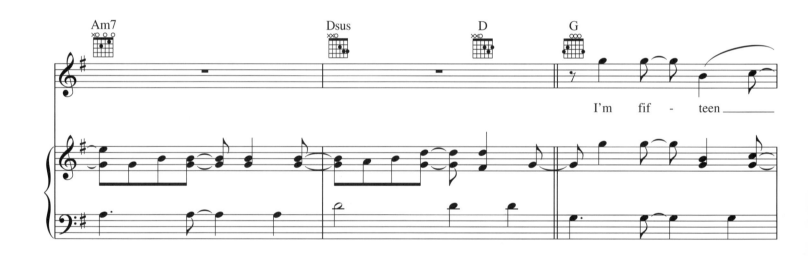

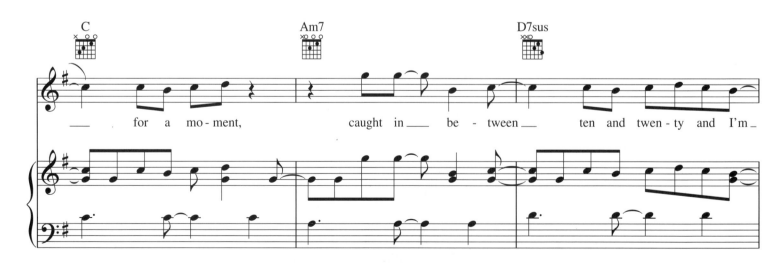

An - oth - er blink of an eye, _ six - ty - sev - en is gone. _ The sun is get - ting high, _

_ we're mov - ing on...

I'm nine - ty - nine _

_ for a mo - ment, I'm dy - ing _ for just _ an - oth - er mo - ment and I'm _

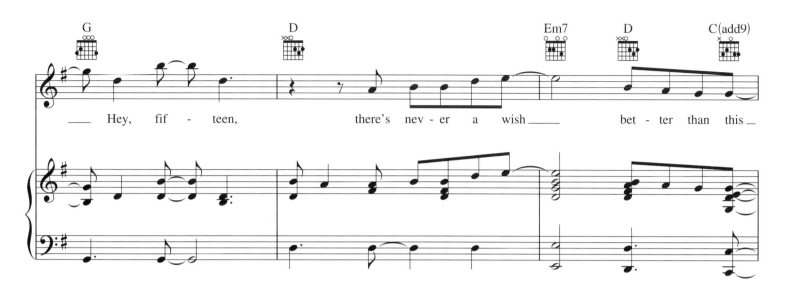

Hey, fif - teen, there's nev - er a wish bet - ter than this

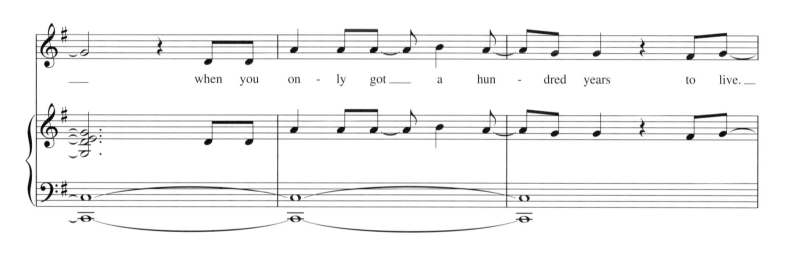

when you on - ly got a hun - dred years to live.

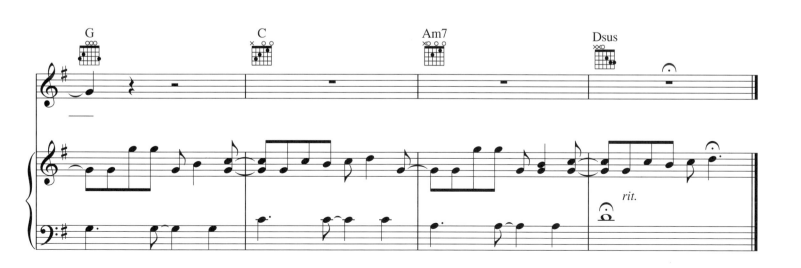

STUPID

Words and Music by
SARAH McLACHLAN

TAKE MY BREATH AWAY
(Love Theme)
from the Paramount Picture TOP GUN

Words and Music by GIORGIO MORODER
and TOM WHITLOCK

SUNRISE

Words and Music by NORAH JONES
and LEE ALEXANDER

Sun - rise, _____ sun - rise, ___ looks like
_____ sur - prise. ___

Piano solo ad lib.

morn - ing in ___ your eyes, ___ but the
find it in ___ your eyes, ___ but I'm

THIS LOVE

Words and Music by ADAM LEVINE
and JESSE CARMICHAEL

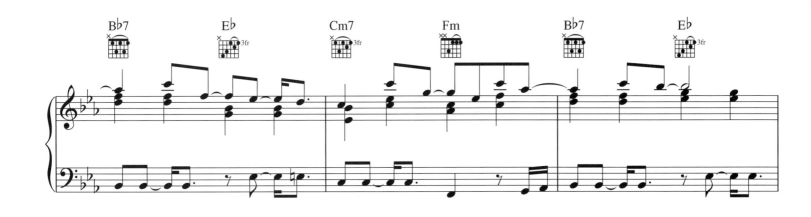

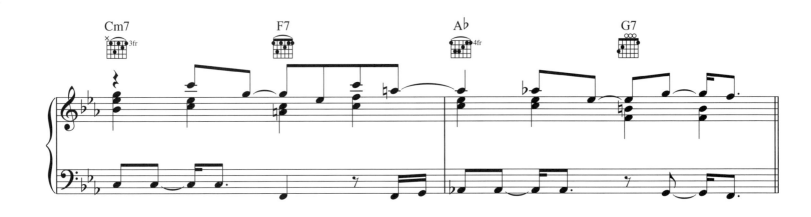

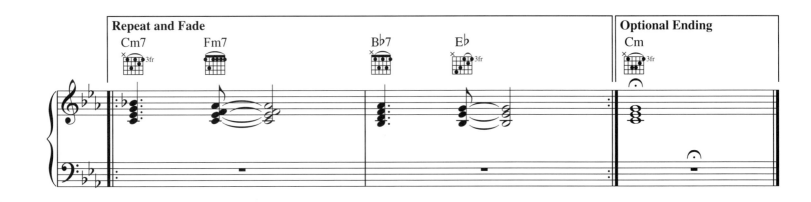

TOXIC

Words and Music by CATHY DENNIS,
CHRISTIAN KARLSSON, PONTUS WINNBERG
and HENRIK JONBACK

Ba - by, can't you see   I'm call - ing.
There's no es - cape.   I can't__ wait.

A guy like you   should wear a warn - ing.   It's dan - ger - ous,
I need a hit.   Ba - by, give me it.   You're dan - ger - ous,

To Coda ⊕

THE WAY YOU MOVE

Words and Music by ANTWAN PATTON,
PATRICK BROWN and CARLTON MAHONE

Moderately, with a groove

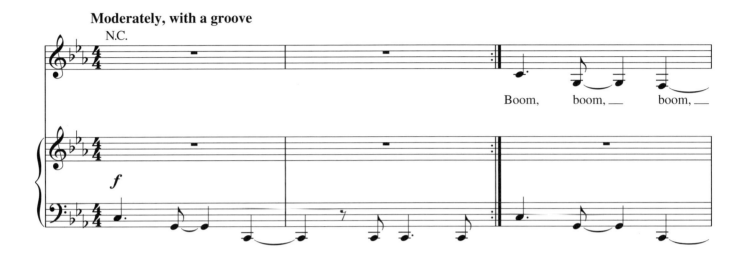

Boom,   boom, ___   boom, ___

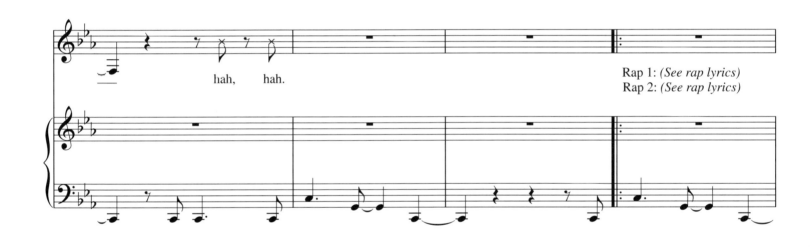

hah,   hah.

Rap 1: (See rap lyrics)
Rap 2: (See rap lyrics)

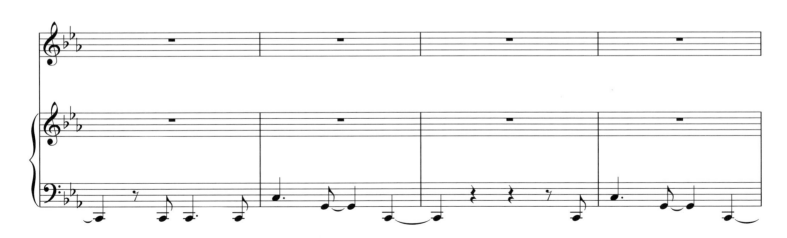

(Rap continues)

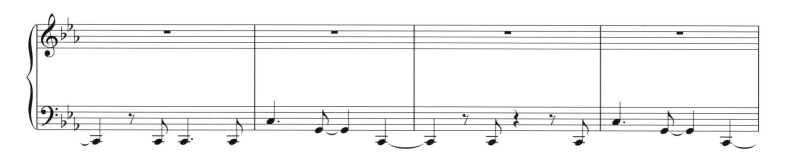

Cm7

I like the way___ you move.___

I like the way___ you move.___

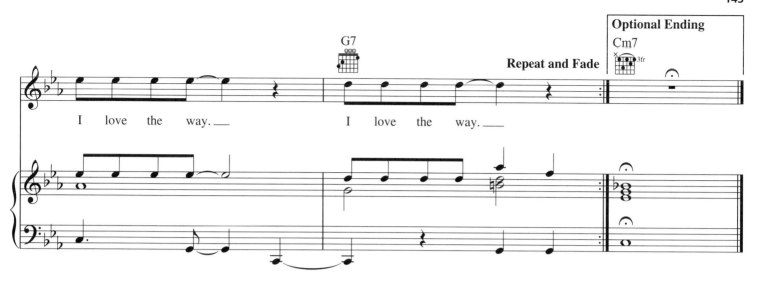

Rap Lyrics

Rap 1:   Ready for action, nip it in the bud.
We never relaxin'. OutKast is everlastin'.
Not clashin', not at all.
But see, my nigga went up to do a little actin'.
Now that's for anyone askin'.
Give me one, pass 'em.
Drip, drip, drop, there goes an eargasm.
Now you comin' out the side of your face.
We tappin' right into your memory banks, thanks.
So click it or ticket, let's see your seatbelt fastened.
Trunk rattlin' like two midgets in the back seat wrestlin'
Speakerboxxx vibrate the tag.
Make it sound like aluminum cans in the bag.
But I know y'all wanted that eight-o-eight.
Can you feel that B-A-S-S, bass?
But I know y'all wanted that eight-o-eight.
Can you feel that B-A-S-S, bass?

Rap 2:   The whole room fell silent. The girls all paused with glee.
Turnin' left, turnin' right, are they lookin' at me?
Well I was lookin' at them, there, there on the dance floor.
Now they got me in the middle feelin' like a man whore.
Especially the big girl. Big girls need love too.
No discrimination here, squirrel. So keep your hands off my cheeks.
Let me study how you ride the beat, you big freak.
Skinny slim women got the the camel-toe within' 'em.
You can hump them, lift them, bend them,
Give them something to remember.
Yell out "timber" when you fall through the chop shop.
Take a deep breath and exhale.
Your ex-male friend, boyfriend was boring as hell.
Well, let me listen to the story you tell.
And we can make moves like a person in jail....
On the low, hoe!

The Ultimate Songbooks!

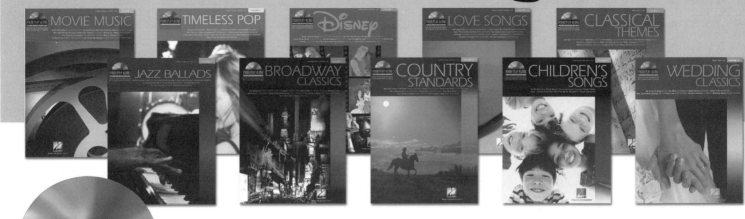

PIANO PLAY-ALONG

These great book/CD packs come with our standard arrangements for piano and voice with guitar chord frames plus a CD. The CD includes a full performance of each song as well as a second track without the piano part so you can play "lead" with the band.

VOLUME 1
MOVIE MUSIC
Come What May • Forrest Gump – Main Title (Feather Theme) • My Heart Will Go On (Love Theme from 'Titanic') • The Rainbow Connection • Tears in Heaven • A Time for Us • Up Where We Belong • Where Do I Begin (Love Theme).
00311072 P/V/G.........................$12.95

VOLUME 2
JAZZ BALLADS
Autumn in New York • Do You Know What It Means to Miss New Orleans • Georgia on My Mind • In a Sentimental Mood • More Than You Know • The Nearness of You • The Very Thought of You • When Sunny Gets Blue.
00311073 P/V/G.........................$12.95

VOLUME 3
TIMELESS POP
Ebony and Ivory • Every Breath You Take • From a Distance • I Write the Songs • In My Room • Let It Be • Oh, Pretty Woman • We've Only Just Begun.
00311074 P/V/G.........................$12.95

VOLUME 4
BROADWAY CLASSICS
Ain't Misbehavin' • Cabaret • If I Were a Bell • Memory • Oklahoma • Some Enchanted Evening • The Sound of Music • You'll Never Walk Alone.
00311075 P/V/G $12.95

VOLUME 5
DISNEY
Beauty and the Beast • Can You Feel the Love Tonight • Colors of the Wind • Go the Distance • Look Through My Eyes • A Whole New World • You'll Be in My Heart • You've Got a Friend in Me.
00311076 P/V/G.........................$12.95

VOLUME 6
COUNTRY STANDARDS
Blue Eyes Crying in the Rain • Crazy • King of the Road • Oh, Lonesome Me • Ring of Fire • Tennessee Waltz • You Are My Sunshine • Your Cheatin' Heart.
00311077 P/V/G $12.95

VOLUME 7
LOVE SONGS
Can't Help Falling in Love • (They Long to Be) Close to You • Here, There and Everywhere • How Deep Is Your Love • I Honestly Love You • Maybe I'm Amazed • Wonderful Tonight • You Are So Beautiful.
00311078 P/V/G.........................$12.95

VOLUME 8
CLASSICAL THEMES
Can Can • Habanera • Humoresque • In the Hall of the Mountain King • Minuet in G Major • Piano Concerto No. 21 in C Major ("Elvira Madigan"), Second Movement Excerpt • Prelude in E Minor, Op. 28, No. 4 • Symphony No. 5 in C Minor, First Movement Excerpt.
00311079 Piano Solo $12.95

VOLUME 9
CHILDREN'S SONGS
Do-Re-Mi • It's a Small World • Linus and Lucy • Sesame Street Theme • Sing • Winnie the Pooh • Won't You Be My Neighbor? (It's a Beautiful Day in This Neigh-borhood) • Yellow Submarine.
0311080 P/V/G $12.95

VOLUME 10
WEDDING CLASSICS
Air on the G String • Ave Maria • Bridal Chorus • Canon in D • Jesu, Joy of Man's Desiring • Ode to Joy • Trumpet Voluntary • Wedding March.
00311081 Piano Solo..................$12.95

VOLUME 11
WEDDING FAVORITES
All I Ask of You • Don't Know Much • Endless Love • Grow Old with Me • In My Life • Longer • Wedding Processional • You and I.
00311097 P/V/G $12.95

VOLUME 12
CHRISTMAS FAVORITES
Blue Christmas • The Christmas Song (Chestnuts Roasting on an Open Fire) • Do You Hear What I Hear • Here Comes Santa Claus (Right down Santa Claus Lane) • I Saw Mommy Kissing Santa Claus • Let It Snow! Let It Snow! Let It Snow! • Merry Christmas, Darling • Silver Bells.
00311137 P/V/G $12.95

VOLUME 13
YULETIDE FAVORITES
Angels We Have Heard on High • Away in a Manger • Deck the Hall • The First Noel • Go, Tell it on the Mountain • Jingle Bells • Joy to the World • O Little Town of Bethlehem.
00311138 P/V/G.........................$12.95

VOLUME 14
POP BALLADS
Have I Told You Lately • I'll Be There for You • It's All Coming Back to Me Now • Looks Like We Made It • Rainy Days and Mondays • Say You, Say Me • She's Got a Way • Your Song.
00311145 P/V/G $12.95

VOLUME 15
FAVORITE STANDARDS
Call Me • The Girl from Ipanema (Garota De Ipanema) • Moon River • My Way • Satin Doll • Smoke Gets in Your Eyes • Strangers in the Night • The Way You Look Tonight.
00311146 P/V/G $12.95

VOLUME 16
TV CLASSICS
The Brady Bunch • Green Acres Theme • Happy Days • Johnny's Theme • Love Boat Theme • Mister Ed • The Munsters Theme • Where Everybody Knows Your Name.
00311147 P/V/G $12.95

VOLUME 17
MOVIE FAVORITES
Back to the Future • Theme from E.T. (The Extra-Terrestrial) • Footloose • For All We Know • Somewhere in Time • Somewhere Out There • Theme from "Terms of Endearment" • You Light Up My Life.
00311148 P/V/G.........................$12.95

VOLUME 18
JAZZ STANDARDS
All the Things You Are • Bluesette • Easy Living • I'll Remember April • Isn't It Romantic? • Stella by Starlight • Tangerine • Yesterdays.
00311149 P/V/G $12.95

VOLUME 19
CONTEMPORARY HITS
Beautiful • Calling All Angels • Don't Know Why • If I Ain't Got You • 100 Years • This Love • A Thousand Miles • You Raise Me Up.
00311162 P/V/G.........................$12.95

VOLUME 20
R&B BALLADS
After the Love Has Gone • All in Love Is Fair • I'll Be There • Let's Stay Together • Midnight Train to Georgia • Say You, Say Me • Tell It Like It Is • Three Times a Lady.
00311163 P/V/G $12.95

Prices, contents and availability subject to change without notice.

FOR MORE INFORMATION, SEE YOUR LOCAL MUSIC DEALER,
OR WRITE TO:

HAL•LEONARD® CORPORATION
7777 W. BLUEMOUND RD. P.O. BOX 13819 MILWAUKEE, WI 53213

Visit Hal Leonard Online at **www.halleonard.com**